THIS BOOK IS

....

THE WORLD'S MOST BORING/SEXY/
DYNAMIC/ROTTEN/UGLY/KISSABLE
STUPID/BEAUTIFUL/LOVABLE/LIBRAN

YOURS IN DISGUST/WITH ALL MY LOVE/
KIND REGARDS ....

P.S. PLEASE TAKE NOTE OF PAGE(S)

....

THE LIBRA BOOK

A CORGI BOOK 0 552 12322 6

First publication in Great Britain
PRINTING HISTORY
Corgi edition published 1983
Corgi edition reissued 1984

Corgi Books are published by Transworld Publishers Ltd.,
Century House, 61-63 Uxbridge Road, Ealing, London W5 5SA.

Made and printed in Great Britain by the
Guernsey Press Co. Ltd., Guernsey, Channel Islands.

THE LIBRA BOOK

BY

IAN HEATH

LIBRA

SEPTEMBER 23 – OCTOBER 22

SEVENTH SIGN OF THE ZODIAC
SYMBOL: THE SCALES
RULING PLANET: VENUS
COLOURS: PASTEL PINK, BLUE
GEMS: TURQUOISE, BLUE OPAL
NUMBER: SIX
DAY: FRIDAY
METAL: COPPER
FLOWER: LILY

...CLIMBS TO TOP OF THE LADDER.....

.......IS HARD-HEADED................

......CAN BE AGGRESSIVE.............

.....WILL WORK ON SUNDAYS........

.......NEEDS A TARGET..............

..... CAN BE UNHELPFUL.............

..... IS A FAST-TALKER..........

.....ALWAYS ON THE 'PHONE..........

.........TAKES RISKS.............

... AND LIKES TO BE WANTED.

EUREKA!
the LIBRAN
finds success as...

......A CLAIRVOYANT..............

.........TEA-TASTER..................

.........TEST-PILOT...................

.........PET-SHOP OWNER...........

.... ASTRONOMER ....

GROOM

...... OR FLORIST.

..... ADORES ORIENTAL RUGS.........

.........READS ROMANTIC NOVELS....

.........TRIES D.I.Y....................

.....IS A BIT OF AN ESCAPIST..........

..... WEARS EXPENSIVE CLOTHES ....

.........OFTEN SNOOZES.............

..... ENJOYS SITTING ON THE LAWN .....

..... MAKES MARMALADE............

...IS AN EARLY RISER...............

....AND LOVES PETS.

...... SNOWBALL FIGHTS ....

. . . . SURFING . . . .

.... PLAYING TENNIS ....

...... EXPENSIVE PERFUMES.........

.... AND FISHING.

the
LIBRAN
dislikes...............

..... RADIO DISC-JOCKEYS..........

.... COWBOY FILMS................

.... DOOR-TO-DOOR SALESMEN........

. . . . QUEUEING . . . .

...PARTY POLITICAL BROADCASTS.......

.........AND B.O.

the
LIBRAN
in love.................

.... CAN'T KEEP IT A SECRET..........

.... LIKES GIVING GIFTS............

..... WEARS SEXY CLOTHES.........

.......IS HIGHLY PASSIONATE.......

.... CAN BE SWEPT OFF FEET..........

.....SOMETIMES DISAGREES..........

..........IS DREAMY..............

......FALLS HEAD-OVER-HEELS.......

......GIVES GENTLE HINTS...........

...AND ENJOYS ROMANTIC EVENINGS.

LIBRAN AND PARTNER

HEART RATINGS

♥♥♥♥♥ WOWEE!!

♥♥♥♥ GREAT, BUT NOT 'IT'

♥♥♥ O.K. — COULD BE FUN

♥♥ FORGET IT

♥ RUN THE OTHER WAY — FAST!

AQUARIUS GEMINI

SCORPIO SAGITTARIUS
LEO VIRGO

ARIES LIBRA CAPRICORN

CANCER

PISCES TAURUS

LIBRA PEOPLE

BRIGITTE BARDOT: BUSTER KEATON
WALTER MATTHAU: OSCAR WILDE
FRANZ LISZT: SARAH BERNHARDT
JULIE ANDREWS: RITA HAYWORTH
F. SCOTT FITZGERALD

JOHN LENNON : GROUCHO MARX
JERRY LEE LEWIS : GORE VIDAL
MARGARET THATCHER : T. S. ELIOT
CLIFF RICHARD : HAROLD PINTER
JOHNNY MATHIS : RICHARD HARRIS
MICKEY ROONEY : RONNIE BARKER
JOHN LE CARRÉ : CHUBBY CHECKER
MAHATMA GANDHI : BILL TIDY
GEORGE GERSHWIN : TREVOR HOWARD
GRAHAM GREENE : CHARLTON HESTON
PIERRE TRUDEAU : ARTHUR MILLER